TRIBE OF PATIENTS

FROM CHIROCANDY MARKETING'S

BILLY STICKER & BRADY STICKER

TRIBE OF PATIENTS

BUILD AN AUDIENCE
OF QUALITY PRACTICE MEMBERS
IN YOUR MARKET

First Edition

ISBN: 978-0-578-67928-0

Table of Contents

VIII

Start Here

Thank you for buying this book. We did want to let you know that this was originally created from a presentation of us teaching this material, which is why it may read different than other books. Our goal was to deliver the best content we could and we do our best teaching talking, not writing.

In the spirit of over delivering, we created a resource page with bonuses and supplemental interviews for every chapter at tribeofpatients.com/bookbonus

Enjoy,

Billy & Brady

What Lead Us Here

"A man must be big enough to admit his mistakes, smart enough to profit from them, and strong enough to correct them." ~John C. Maxwell

A Word From Billy

I started in chiropractic as the director of marketing for a multi-practice chiropractic office. I did their marketing; then I started doing their Day 1 and Day 2s, including financials and closing them on care plans. The only thing I didn't do was adjust. Back then, we used the Pro-Adjuster so I probably could have figured that out! Long story short, I fell in love with the profession.

Then I founded ChiroCandy Marketing, a coaching community for chiropractors and functional medicine practitioners, which started as a podcast (Chirocandy. com). I was also helping chiropractors write books. One day, a client asked, "Have you ever ran Facebook ads?" We tested Facebook marketing for him and he got over 50 leads in the very first month. He started referring people to us. Since then, we have managed over four million dollars in paid ads for local chiropractors. Now, ChiroCandy Marketing is one of the largest chiropractic marketing agency in the profession.

Since then, we have worked for the ICA and we are Power Partners with AMPED. We have been featured in Chiropractic Philanthropist and Circle of Docs. I have published articles in Chiro Economics and spoken at ChiroSushi, Parker Dallas and a host of other events. I have even traveled to speak to doctors at events in London and Paris.

I am an established author and have published four books:

1. Achieving Massive Business Growth: Proven Marketing Strategies To Grow Your Business And Dominate Your Competition
2. 3 Simple Steps For Marketing Your Local Business Online
3. The ABC's Of A Leader: Principles For Making A Difference
4. Profit Practice 2.0: A Marketer's Guide For Growing Your Chiropractic Practice

We have also created a system to help chiropractors write a book, which can help them to market their practice (www.chirocandymarketing.com/book-vsl).

Finally, I'm very fortunate and blessed to have won not one, but two, 2-Comma Club Awards through ClickFunnels for what we do in the chiropractic and functional medicine profession.

My heart is to help chiropractors better deliver their message to their communities.

Billy Sticker
chirocandymarketing.com

A Word From Brady

In junior high, I remember taking an aptitude test and my top career suggestion was marketing (I guess you can say I get it honestly). That day, after school I ran into the house saying, "Dad, guess what! This test said I'd do great in marketing. How cool would it be if one day we had a marketing company together?!"

Fast forward almost 10 years and here we are, running one of the largest marketing agencies in the chiropractic profession.

Way back then, I didn't have any intentions to work in the chiropractic profession. I had really wanted to go into ministry. After high school, I completed a two-year Bible college program at Christ For The Nations Institute in Dallas, Texas. I then transferred to Dallas Baptist University and graduated with a bachelor's in Marketing.

Since then I've gotten married to my high school sweetheart, Sara, built our dream home, and even helped launch Vibrant Church, in The Woodlands, Texas. I currently serve here as Student Pastor. I am

5

blessed to be able to serve in ministry and still run things at ChiroCandy Marketing.

While still living in Dallas, I attended a conference with my dad, Billy, and heard Dr. Gilles Lamarche for the first time. It was then that a light turned on. I had been helping run the agency side of ChiroCandy, but after Dr. Gilles' presentation, I fully understood what a powerful message chiropractors had to share.

I even briefly considered attending Parker in Dallas. After some thought, I realized I have a greater impact on the profession running ChiroCandy Marketing than I would if I just owned my own practice.

How to Make the Best Use of This Book

"Eighty percent of success is showing up."
~Woody Allen

I suggest you start by reading this book from start to end. Just read. Don't take notes or anything.

Then go through the book again and take notes and make a checklist for yourself.

Finally, start with the first chapter and do all the action steps. Then go on to the second chapter and so on.

The best way to learn is to take action. Make sure to visit tribeofpatients.com/bookbonus for extra content.

Part I

Chapter 1

THE TIME IS NOW

"The purpose of a storyteller is not to tell you how to think, but to give you questions to think upon."
~Brandon Sanderson

The Time is Now

"If there was ever a moment to follow your passion and do work that matters, this is it." ~Seth Godin

I honestly believe we have never had a better opportunity to be in practice. Even though I'm not a chiropractor or healthcare practitioner, I'm telling you, there has never been a better time to dominate in your local market.

If you don't have enough clients, it's because most people in your area don't know what you do. The solution to this problem is to use social media, such as Facebook, Instagram and YouTube.

Social media marketing has proved to be the most effective way to find your ideal new patients. These are the people who actually show up for services and who want what it is that you do. In this book, you'll learn how to find your ideal patients who will know you, like you, and trust you. Not only that, they will also know **what** you do, **how** you do it and **why** you do it.

We call this building a *Tribe of Patients.*

Action steps

"You can't steer a parked car." ~Tim Elmore

In the rest of this book, you'll learn how to dominate social media marketing and build your dream practice, with dream patients, without having to discount your services. Make sure to visit tribeofpatients.com/bookbonus for extra content.

Chapter 2

STOP FOCUSING ON LEADS

"Approach each customer with the idea of helping him or her solve a problem or achieve a goal, not of selling a product or service." ~Brian Tracy

My goal in this chapter is to change your mindset about leads. Have you read the bestselling book, *Seven Habits of Highly Effective People* by Stephen Covey? In it, he talks about a key concept called a paradigm shift. The story he uses to demonstrate it was very transformational for me.

The story is about a man sitting in a waiting room in a doctor's office. His children are running wild—

climbing over things, tearing up magazines—but he's not paying any attention to them. The rest of the patients in the waiting room are getting more and more impatient and irritated.

Finally, one of them says, "Excuse me, sir. Your children are being a little bit of a distraction. Please could you calm them down?" The man looks up and he's very apologetic and says, "I'm so sorry. My wife died a couple of days ago. They just lost their mom, so they are not themselves."

That information changed everyone's paradigm of how they viewed the situation. That's what I want to do. I want you to have a paradigm shift on what "leads" are when it comes to marketing.

Now, if your goal is to be in practice in your town for the next one to two years, you know what, you probably need to focus on leads. But if you plan on planting your flag and establishing yourself as a pillar in your community, then you need to stop focusing on leads and focus on something else.

Facebook leads suck!

"Clarity comes from engagement, not thought"
~Marie Forleo

If you have done any marketing on social media before, chances are you or your staff have noted that Facebook leads can be poor quality. This is because of the mindset of Facebook users.

Whenever we say Facebook, we are including Instagram. If you don't know, Instagram is owned by Facebook. Anything that we do on Facebook, you can push a button and send it over to Instagram as well. If you are making a regular post, you can do the same thing on Instagram and post it to your Facebook Page. So when it comes to paid marketing, whenever we say Facebook, just know that it's a big umbrella that covers Instagram as well.

Facebook and Screenings

"Don't judge each day by the harvest you reap but by the seeds that you plant." ~Robert Louis Stevenson

No one is going to the Bridal Expo this weekend, hoping to find a chiropractor but you and I both know that across the country, there are going to be chiropractors set up doing screenings.

Do they work? As you know, I used to as a marketing director for a multi-practice chiropractic office. I used to manage these different events. People are walking down your row. They are looking at whatever the theme of the event is but then they see you. Then the wife is elbowing her husband, "Look, there's a chiropractor." They stop at your booth and so do a few other people. If you have 20 people stop at your booth that weekend, you are hoping to get maybe six of them or so to come into your office over the next week or two. **You have to work the numbers.**

It's the same thing on Facebook. No one is going to Facebook looking for you. That's what Google is for. If people want a chiropractor, they go to Google and type in "Chiropractor near me." However, you can still generate tons of quality leads on Facebook if you do it right. The key is to get your message out there so it's just like screenings and you have to work the numbers.

Leads better than referrals

"Quality is never an accident. It is always the result of intelligent efforts." ~John Ruskin

Usually, your favorite new patients are the ones that are referred by your patients. What if I could show you a system to generate leads that are better than referrals?

Think about it. When a referral comes in, you still have to leverage the relationship between you and the person who has been referred. However, when people come in after watching your videos, there's no need to leverage your relationship because they feel they already have a relationship with you.

To get leads that are better than referrals, you have to learn these three steps:

- How to make viral videos that establish you as the go-to authority in your community.
- How to drastically increase the show-up rate of your leads using this little-known tip

- How to always be retargeting—why to retarget and how to do it.

Action steps

"Content is the fuel for your lead generation efforts."
~Dayna Rothman

- Are you willing to make a paradigm shift?
- Will you agree to be coachable and do the work if I pull back the curtain and show you how to get those high-quality leads?

I hope you replied with a resounding "Yes."

In the rest of the book, I will describe exactly how you can get a steady stream of high-quality leads to your office.

Make sure to visit tribeofpatients.com/bookbonus for extra content.

Chapter 3

Marketing Fundamentals

"Our goal is to be deliberately sought out again and again for our service, our values and the way we empower and impact the people we serve."

~Bernadette Jiwa

I have been an avid student of marketing for several years now and if you have studied marketing at all, chances are you have heard of Dan Kennedy. He is known as the godfather of direct response marketing. If you haven't, I highly recommend that you read his books or follow his audio or video training. One of Dan Kennedy's most important concepts is the marketing triangle.

The Marketing Triangle
(Market, Message, Media)

"Always enter the conversation already occurring in

the customer's mind." ~Dan Kennedy

Dan Kennedy's Marketing Triangle consists of three basic components:

- Market
- Message
- Media

Market

This is your ideal patient. Who is it you are trying to reach? You have to know and define your ideal patient. Many of you will say, "Everyone is a customer," but that's not true. If you try to appeal to everyone, you just end up appealing to no one. And if you don't address the right person in the right way, your message will fall flat and it won't give you the results you want.

Message

What is the message that you want to get to your ideal clients? You need something desirable that will appeal to that specific type of person. Match your message to their pain points, fears, passions, hopes and dreams.

Media

What media are you going to use to deliver your message? You have got many types of media: newspapers, magazines, direct mail, TV, radio, and internet. In this book, we are going to focus on online marketing and specifically, social media marketing.

We need to make sure that we focus on all three parts of the marketing triangle because all three of them are important. If you leave out any one of them, you are going to struggle.

I already said that this is the greatest time in history to be in practice. In fact, it's the best time to have any kind of business because social media levels the playing field.

The modern marketing revolution

"It is no longer enough to satisfy your customers. You must delight them." ~Philip Kotler

Think about marketing even 20 years ago. (The older I get, the shorter time 20 years seems to be.) Imagine a marketing executive in a meeting saying, "Instead of doing advertising on billboard or radio or television, what if we could somehow develop some kind of device that people would carry around with them. A device that they would look at all the time—when they're standing in line or going to the restroom or sitting at the dinner table or visiting with their family.

22

We could deliver our message to them through this device and even get them addicted to it."

I don't know if they would go that far in real life and but that's what has actually happened.

It's funny, we still call them phones but they do so much more than that. I heard somebody say, "It's like calling your car a cup holder. Yeah, your car has a cup holder in it but it does so much more." So yes, your smartphone is a phone but it does so much more. Because of the power of social media, you can deliver your message to your ideal client through their phone.

You can build what everybody calls the "know, like and trust factor." People begin to know who you are, they begin to like you and they begin to trust you but not only that, you can tell them what you do, why you do it and how you do it. It can dramatically change your practice.

But you have to understand that people get on social media not to look for you but to do stuff with family and friends. They post pictures with friends, they check up on their grandkids or do goofy pictures with their pets. That's what people use social media for. It's different.

Marketing on Facebook is a little bit different than what you would do on radio, TV or even on YouTube. You have to make sure you have the proper mindset. You have to enter the conversation that your ideal patient is already having in their head. Let's take a deeper dive into it. Before we do that, let's look at some basic marketing principles. The first is the AIDA formula. You have probably heard of it before.

The AIDA Formula

AIDA is what I like to refer to as the **Marketing What.**

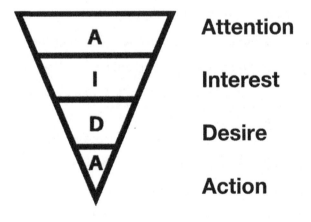

Attention

Interest

Desire

Action

Here's the AIDA formula in a nutshell:

- **Attention:** Get the attention of your ideal clients
- **Interest:** Tell them something interesting, useful or entertaining.
- **Desire:** Make them desire your services and products
- **Action:** Get them to take action

The AIDA Formula in action

On Facebook, we tell you to use props in your videos, for example, a spine. If you have a model spine in your hand, it may be normal for you but it's not normal for others. They are scrolling through their newsfeed and it gets their attention. They read the headline, they see what else is going on in the video. Then we're able to create some interest, next, a strong desire, and finally, we get them to take a specific action. So you have to keep this in mind: Attention, Interest, Desire and Action. This is what we want to do with our marketing.

The PAST Formula

The PAST formula is what I like to refer to as the **Marketing How.**

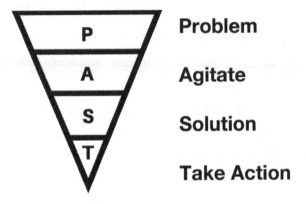

P — **Problem**

A — **Agitate**

S — **Solution**

T — **Take Action**

If you have subscribed to our podcast, I have taught the PAST formula for several years now.

- **Problem**
- **Agitate**
- **Solution**
- **Take Action**

You address the problem, agitate that problem, lay out the solution and then get them to take action. Once you grab their attention, you go from interest to desire and get them to take action by following this formula.

You can follow this formula in your day ones and day twos. You can use it in your workshops, whether it's a ***Dinner with the Doc*** or an in-office workshop. You can even follow the PAST formula while writing a book. Address the problem and agitate that problem in the first part of the book. Then lay out the solution to that problem and what action your clients need to take in the remaining part of the book.

The PAST Formula in action

Back in 2012 after a head-on motor vehicle accident, I was diagnosed with a Chiari malformation type 1. I didn't have any symptoms until the accident. When I went to the gym and picked up a dumbbell, I would get extreme tingling in my forearms. I went to a neurologist and he referred me to a neurosurgeon.

Well, I have worked with chiropractors enough to know that there was probably something wrong with my neck so I had a CT scan. I was diagnosed with a Chiari malformation type 1. It was obvious that I needed to have a Chiari decompression surgery.

I ended up going to see Dr. Dong Kim in Houston. He's the doctor who took care of Gabrielle Giffords, the member of Congress, who was shot in Arizona. She was shot in the head and she survived. Her husband was an astronaut so they brought her to Houston. The main reason was to be closer to him but also because Houston is known for its exceptional medical community.

Dr. Dong Kim specializes in Chiari malformation decompression surgery. When I went to consult him, one of the first things he did was fantastic from a marketing standpoint. When we made the appointment, they sent us the paperwork online. Along with the paperwork, they also emailed a webinar. They said that Dr. Kim requires all of his patients to watch this webinar before they come in, which as a marketer, I thought, "This is fantastic."

Then they called to confirm a day or two in advance if I was going to make the appointment. When I said yes, they asked if I had watched the webinar. "Yes, I have," I replied. Once I got there that morning,

"Hey, Mr. Sticker, glad you're here." I said, "Thank you," and handed them all the paperwork. Then they asked again, "Okay, have you watched the webinar?"

That's a great example of Dr. Kim educating his patients before they even walked in the door.

When I got in there, Dr. Kim came out and he followed this PAST formula to a T. He addressed the problem and basically said, "Okay, since the accident, since you started having symptoms, they have gotten progressively worse, correct?"

I replied, "Yes."

Then he laid out the solution, "Well, I see this all the time. Now, that you're having symptoms, they're going to continue to get worse." So he addressed the problem, now he was agitating it and then he kind of sat back and said, "But listen, this is why you're here. This is what we do. You are young; we can address this now. You should make a full recovery and then you have the rest of your life to never worry about this again."

Finally, he said, "Okay, I have got March 3rd available as my next open date for surgery, is that good with you?" So he got us to take action right away. It's just a great example of using this PAST formula.

First deliver what they want, then what they need

"People don't want to be sold.
What people do want is news and information about the things they care about." ~Larry Weber

Finally, let's discuss guru marketing training. If you are interested in marketing, you may have read many books on marketing. For example, you may be following top marketers like Ryan Deiss, Russell Brunson, Frank Kern, Pat Flynn, and John Lee Dumas. All of them have seven- or eight-figure internet marketing businesses. I'm friends with some of them.

However, if you follow everything that they teach, it can be a problem because all of them are selling how to make money online. It's easy for them to sell their products or courses because people are looking for money-making products. However, if you try to follow their strategies, you may not be as successful. That's because people aren't necessarily looking for healthcare or wellness care. It's easier to sell people what they want than to sell them what they need.

For example, most chiropractors want to build a practice full of wellness care. They want people to come in for life and build this huge practice based on wellness. The problem is, you can't sell that on the front end. Nobody wants to commit to a lifetime of wellness care because they don't know what it is.

It's easier to sell people what they want than to sell them what they need. So you have to ask yourself, "What do my ideal patients want?" Then you have to market what they want and when they come in, deliver what they want as well as what they need.

This is a very crucial mindset that you need to have. Market what they want and deliver what they want. Then educate them and deliver what they need.

Action steps

If you want people to buy your products,
your products have to become part of their environment."
~Eric McFadden

1. **Create your personal Marketing Triangle**
   - What is my market (my ideal client)?
   - What is my message to my ideal client?
   - Where are the places that my ideal clients hang out?

2. **The AIDA Formula – The Marketing What**
   - **Attention:** What do I have to do to get the attention of my ideal clients?
   - **Interest:** What do they find interesting, useful or entertaining?
   - **Desire:** What will make them desire my services and products?
   - **Action:** What do I have to do to get them to take action?

3. **The PAST Formula – The Marketing How**
   - **Problem:** How can I define the biggest problem of my ideal clients?

- **Agitate:** How do I agitate that problem?
- **Solution:** How do I identify the most effective solution for that problem?
- **Take Action:** How do I get them to take action?

4. **Deliver what they want, then what they need**

- What do my ideal patients want right now?
- What are their real long-term needs?

Make sure to visit tribeofpatients.com/bookbonus for extra content.

Chapter 4

The Problem With the "$21 Facebook Offer"

"If you are not taking care of your customer, your competitor will." ~Bob Hooey

Many chiropractors don't want to run any kind of discounted offer on Facebook because they think it only brings in low-quality leads. While there is some truth to that, Facebook did not create the "$21 Offer." People have been doing offers for a very long time. Back before the Facebook & Instagram ads craze, Chiropractors offered discounted exams at screenings, health talks, etc. Well if offers work so great at screenings, why do they only bring in the low-quality tire-kicker leads from Facebook ads?

Context

The reason why the $21 offer doesn't always get great results from Facebook ads is that the offer is out of context.

Let's go back to the example of a screening. People don't go to the farmers market or bridal expo to look for a chiropractor. However, I guarantee you every weekend there's probably a chiropractor set up at a local farmers market or bridal expo. Facebook is the exact same way. People don't go to Facebook looking for a chiropractor, but if you play your cards right, you can still get some new patients from it.

If you were to set up a booth at the farmers market and stand on the table with a megaphone screaming, "Attention _____ area! I'm Dr. John Smith and I'm doing something CRAZY to promote my chiropractic office! I'm giving away 25 vouchers for a $21 Exam."

People would look at you like you are crazy. You would never market yourself like that out in public, at a screening, or a half talk. So why would you market yourself like that online?

Content

If you look at how new patient acquisition works at a screening; someone might walk up to your booth and you start a conversation with them. You ask them what symptoms they might be having, and explain a little bit more of what you do, and how you do it in the office. You start a dialogue, you're authentic, and you begin to build a relationship where this potential new patient starts to know, like, and trust you.

A relationship starts to form because some trust has been built with the perceived value of the service you provide. This is when you introduce the offer.

That's when you go in and say "I really feel like we can help you. If you were to just walk into my office off the street, your initial exam would cost $121. But if you sign up here, it's only $21."

That's how chiropractors all across the United States get new patients every weekend at screenings.

Now here lies the big question:

How can we replicate that online?

The biggest mistake we typically see chiropractors make whenever they are running ads online is all they promote is a new patient special offer. Now, as we discovered, there's nothing specifically wrong with running a new patient special offer. The problem is the offer is just out of context.

The great thing about Facebook, Instagram, and Google is that we are able to keep track of who has been to our website, engaged with our social media page, and/or watched any of our video content.

Call To Action

Instead of just taking a "$21 Facebook Offer" and blanketing that offer to everyone in your town, what if you just focused on showing that offer to the people that have watched your video content, engaged with your social media pages, or have been to your website?

That is how you replicate the process of getting a new patient at a screening online.

You do that with retargeting. It's just like how Amazon does their advertising strategy.

Let's say you go to Amazon and look at flat-screen TVs, for example. You scroll through their site and look at all of the different options. Then, later that day you go to Facebook and then guess what! You see Amazon ads showing you the TVs you were looking at. Amazon could easily take that ad with all of the TVs and just show it to all of America. Amazon could think "TV's are great! Everyone could benefit from a new TV." Instead, they only show that ad to people they know are looking to buy.

Chiropractors are the exact same way. We talk to plenty of docs that say, "I want everyone to see our ads! Everyone can benefit from chiropractic care!" While yes, I agree that everyone can benefit from chiropractic care. However, when you just blanket your "$21 offer" ad to everyone in your town, all you're doing is attracting people that are looking for a discount. These people aren't really looking to start care. They're looking for a good deal.

That's why not many chiropractors advertise on Groupon. It doesn't bring people in on a NEED basis. It brings people in on an "I want a discount" basis.

Your goal with your marketing should be to:

- Raise the perceived value of what you have to offer
- Be Authentic
- Get your viewers to know, like, and trust you
- Teach what you do, why you do it and how you do it

Then make an offer for them to come into your office.

Part II

Chapter 5

Building Authority With Videos

"Business decision makers LOVE online video because it gives them the most amount of information in the shortest amount of time." ~Robert Weiss

The first step is how to make viral videos that establish you as the go-to authority in your community.

I want you to think about your favorite practice members. The ones that get you and your team excited because they bring a certain positive spirit and enthusiasm into the office when they come in. These are the members who have been educated and who understand what you do, why you do it, and how you do it.

Effective patient education

"No matter what you do, your job is to tell your story." ~Gary Vaynerchuk

Most offices begin the education of their patients on their day one, day two or after report of findings. **What if you started to educate your patients 2 weeks or even 2 months before they came in?** This is what I call the secret sauce. You have a life-changing message and it's up to you to deliver that message.

There are people driving past your office right now. And they want what it is you do. The problem is they don't know what you do. They think it is back pain relief and neck pain relief. But there is so much more that you do!

As we already mentioned, Facebook marketing is a lot like screenings. Your ideal practice members are on Facebook and other social media. It's up to you to reach them and educate them.

Story of an acute doctor

"It's not what you upload, it's the strategy with which you upload." ~Will Keenan

Here's a great example.

We had an office call one day. It was from a chiropractor and he said, "Listen, I'm a chiropractor here in Texas and we are an integrated office. We do some medical stuff also. However, everyone gets adjusted. We are fantastic at chiropractic. We have a seven-figure clinic but there's some new guy down the street, that just graduated, just opened his office and every time I turn around, he has a different video on Facebook. It's driving me crazy. He doesn't even know how to adjust yet. I know this because we see some of his patients. He doesn't need to be all over Facebook; we need to be all over Facebook!"

He had watched one video that this new chiropractor in town had posted on Facebook and that put him in a retargeting audience. Retargeting on Facebook means, "If somebody has watched 25 to 50% of this video, put them in another audience and retarget them."

So whenever the new chiropractor recorded a new video, he saw it in his feed. This happened week after week, and it created the impression that this other chiropractor was everywhere in his town. It was driving him insane.

We want to do the same thing for you

"Marketing is no longer about the stuff that you make, but about the stories you tell." ~Seth Godin

For example, Dr. Michael is a client who's been with us for about three years or so. He's a fantastic guy and one of our favorite clients. He was one of the first offices for whom we used video marketing instead of any kind of discounted offer. The first video he did was a newborn getting adjusted. It was a fantastic video and we targeted women, 30 years and older.

Then Dr. Michael did a general video on a new patient getting an adjustment. He did a video on Bulletproof Coffee. Then he posted a video of him standing in front of a whiteboard with a spine in his hand and explaining cervical issues and headaches. All of these videos had great content. Once he started working with us, he had to hire a new associate because his practice grew so much.

Now, ideally, we like to see offices do videos once a week. Dr. Michael was doing them about every other week but in three months, he had built a retargeting audience of 9,000 people in this town that had watched at least 25 to 50% of these videos.

Okay, what if he just stopped right here? What if he never targeted a cold audience again and just focused on the 9,000 people who have stopped what they were doing and watched some of his videos? How many of those 9,000 people does he need to totally transform his practice?

Think about it. These are people who know what it is he does. They know why he does it and how he does it. They know, like and trust him. This is how you build an audience of people who come in. They think they already know you.

The power of consistent content

You can earn attention by creating something interesting and valuable and then publishing it online for free." ~David Meerman Scott

There have been several times where I've been out speaking and somebody walks up to me and wants to introduce themselves because they've been listening to our *ChiroCandy* podcast for the past several years (chirocandy.com). It's a special honor and I don't take it lightly.

I was in an event in Atlanta one weekend. Two people walked up to me even though I was not t speaker at that event. They had never met me before but they just wanted to shake my hand because they have been following me so they felt they knew me.

One day, I was talking with Dr. George Curry, the president of the ICA (International Chiropractors Association). We were at a big event and a couple of people had stopped and interrupted us to shake his hand and talk to him. Then somebody walked up and said, "I'm so sorry to interrupt you guys…" and I stepped out of the way thinking he wants to talk to Dr. Curry but he says to me, "Billy, I've been a fan of yours for several years now. I have to leave but I didn't want to leave without meeting you, introducing myself and shaking your hand."

That felt really good and it's because I have built that authority by delivering consistent content. Now, when those people interact with me, they feel they already know me. You can do the same in your community by posting videos.

Video content ideas

"Video is an effective form of communication that needs to be integrated into each and every aspect of your existing marketing efforts." ~James Wedmore

Now let's talk about the different types of content that you can do.

You can do **condition-specific videos**, for example, migraine or sports injuries. We call this the PAST

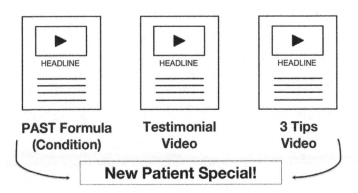

formula where you address the problem, agitate it, lay out the solution and then tell them to take action.

In these online content videos, we don't want you to have a very big call to action at the end. Don't talk about cervical issues and headaches for 60 to 90 seconds and then put on your mattress salesman hat in the last 20 seconds and tell them about a special offer for which they have to come in by Monday.

If you do this, you'll lose credibility. No one else in the healthcare profession does that, so don't do it. Instead, you would have a landing page set up separately and you just put a link to it in your description.

Here's a little bonus marketing tip for you. Always give them a clear path on what to do next.

Even though you are not trying to sell directly in your content video, you can end with something like, "Listen. If you're having headaches or someone you know is having headaches, we'd love to see if we can help. Go ahead and call the office and let's see what we can do." That's all you need to say. Then you can have a link in the description of the video that says, "New patients, click here to schedule an appointment."

When they click the link, they don't have to go back to your Facebook page to try to hunt down your phone number. There's a clear path on what to do next if they resonate with that video and want to take action now.

Even if they don't click on the link, it's okay because we are going to retarget them and show them a testimonial video or maybe a three tips video. There are all kinds of stuff that you can do and then you can send them to some kind of new-patient special offer. Does it have to be a discounted offer? No.

For example, Dr. Travis had a landing page set up that simply said, "Dr. Travis is now accepting new patients. Click here to schedule an appointment." They would click on the link and fill the form and that's all they had to do.

More content ideas for videos

"Content comes in many forms; we tend to think of written content when the term is used, but the reality is, video and image content can be more useful when it comes to influencing search and social results."
~Debra Mastaler

You can do an online workshop and break that into pieces or advertise for a workshop. We got this idea from Dr. Josh Axe's Natural Solutions for XYZ—headaches, sciatica, low back pain, etc. Whatever the disorder, "Natural Solutions" is a title that gets great results.

You can also do videos on what to eat, what not to eat, and so on. For example, when you go to a local restaurant in your town, you can post a video where you say, "Hey, guys, whenever we talk about nutrition in the office, a lot of our practice members share how they make great decisions when they are eating at home but they struggle when they go out to eat. Here I am at XYZ restaurant and this is one of our favorites. Chances are you guys eat here too. I just wanted to show you some healthy choices that you can make here."

Then, you show what you are ordering or eating. Then you can get that restaurant to share that video on their page and now you start to build an audience of not just your people but also of theirs and you get to retarget all of these people.

Another idea that works really well is to post a series of videos on the same topic. For example, The Top Five Questions New Patients Ask. You can do five different videos right there. Then you can do a video series on The Top Five Questions You Wish a New Patient Would Ask.

Action steps

"The amount of information contained in one single frame can take 3 pages to describe. The feeling, the colors, the message is seen immediately.

It is a known fact that people engage more when they watch a video and tend to stay watching it. They are also happy to pass it along. Video informs and entertains people and, good or bad, today most people prefer to watch a video rather than read a page of text."

~Lisa Lubin

(three-time Emmy Award-winning producer)

Change your mindset about posting video content on Facebook and other platforms.

Here are the most effective types of videos you can create:

- Conditions (Headaches/cervical conditions)
- Online Workshops (Natural solutions for...)
- Trauma, Toxins and Negative Thoughts
- Top Five Questions New Patients Ask
- Top Five Question I Wish Patients Would Ask

We have about 50 sample videos in our training portal for our clients. We also have a PDF report containing a list of many different content ideas for your videos. Make sure to visit tribeofpatients.com/bookbonus for extra content on this topic.

Chapter 6

Professional vs iPhone Videos

"Small deeds done are better than great deeds planned." ~Peter Marshall

As small business owners, we oftentimes think our content and the way we are perceived online needs to be top of the line professional. We think our videos need to be polished and super high quality. If you look at these really big brands, Coca-Cola, Amazon, Apple, you would never in a million years see them post a selfie video recorded on an iPhone. So why would we do that?

After working with over 400 offices and managing millions of dollars in advertising spending, I believe that cell phone videos actually might be a better fit for you and your office whenever it comes to your marketing.

Now, if you're an Android user, just a fair warning. We use the term "iPhone video" several times throughout this chapter. Don't worry, you can still use androids to record videos.

If we look at these big brands like Coca-Cola, Apple, and Amazon, these are giant corporations. Now us as small businesses, especially if you are a one doctor office, need to have a different mindset. Whenever it comes to small businesses, more often than not, people are going to be a lot more likely to buy from a person than a brand. So if you are the owner, you need to be the face of the brand.

Now let's talk about the difference between professional videos and videos just recorded on a cell phone. I believe that there is a time and place for both of them.

Professional Videos

Professional videos will have post-production editing done. These videos are typically 1080p or 4K quality video. For comparison, the flatscreen in my living room is a 4K TV. It's a super high-quality video. 9 times out of 10 it's going to be scripted from a teleprompter, where you're just reading a script word for word. Equipment for this would be expensive cameras, lights, microphones, and editing software. You will probably have your office logo or graphics, or phone number down at the bottom of the screen. Maybe the beginning of the video has an animation with your logo. You probably have to pay someone hundreds or thousands of dollars to edit it. A lot of times there is background music. These are great for TV commercials or to put on the front page of your website.

iPhone Videos

There is not a whole lot of post-production editing needed with these videos. A lot of times these are going to be closer to 720p, which is still considered HD (high definition), but nowadays you can get up to

4K video with iPhones. You can go into your camera settings to make sure you are recording videos on 4K at 24 frames per second. This will give you good quality videos. These would be more off the cuff, without a word-for-word script. You could prep by making a short outline with a few bullet points, and probably get it done in one or two takes. You do not have to do a whole lot of cuts or editing. Just film, post on social media, and then done. Super low-barrier to entry.

With iPhone videos, you will come across as more authentic. You are not super stiff, sounding like a robot reading from a teleprompter. People are used to iPhone videos. They have hundreds of them saved to their phone's camera roll. If you scroll through Facebook or Instagram right now, 9/10 of the videos were just shot on a phone and then uploaded straight to the platform. When you use iPhone videos, you end up coming across as approachable because you are mimicking the exact same content that people are used to seeing.

People are turned off by the overproduced, professional videos. Let's say I'm scrolling through

Facebook and I see a video that's super, super professional. It looks like a TV commercial with background music, logo animations and a phone number at the bottom of the screen. I'm going to automatically think, "oh, this is an ad." And then I'm going to keep scrolling. People do not want to 'get sold something'. People want authenticity.

If I see a video that's shot on an iPhone with the headline, "The TRUTH about Headaches & Migraines", and I'm someone that gets frequent headaches. I'm going to be a lot more prone to stop scrolling and watch that video. I do not feel like the person in the video is trying to sell me something. However, if I see a professional video with the same headline; with background music, crystal clear video, the phrase "Call us now 555-555-5555" at the bottom of the screen, I'm automatically going to think, "Alright, what are they trying to sell me?" I'm going to be expecting a bait-and-switch.

And let's face it, you're a chiropractor, not a video editor. Even though you probably do it with the best intentions; adding background music, logo animations, etc. It's probably going to come across as cringy. It's still not going to be the same as if you paid someone else to do it professionally.

There's nothing wrong with wanting to come across as professional. You can spend $50 on amazon and get a ring light and lapel mic that will plug up straight into your phone. Other than that, just focus on the quality of the content rather than the actual video quality itself.

Do not feel like you need to make your own TV commercial for every video on Facebook. Not only is it going to be a little bit cringe or salesy, but it's also not going to perform as well as an authentic video shot on a cellphone.

Chapter 7

How to Drastically Increase Show-Up Rates

"The mobile phone is used from when you get up in the morning and is often the last thing you interact with at night." ~Jan Chipchase

We are going to discuss a little known tip to drastically increase the show-up rate of your leads.

When it comes to marketing on Facebook, roughly 30% show up. So if ten people click on your Facebook ad and fill in their name, email, and phone number, only three of them will walk in the door.

However, some of our offices see a show-up rate of around 60%, which is double the normal rate. Those are typically the offices that are doing videos and have built a really warm audience. It dramatically increases the show-up rate of those leads. You can do targeted surveys and other strategies to get high-quality leads. But if you really want to boost your show-up rate, you need to do videos.

Spam calls and spam emails

According to the YouMail Robocall Index, 58.5 billion robocalls were made in 2019.

And 9.6 billion robocalls were placed nationwide so far in 2020, equaling roughly 29.1 calls per person affected.

So people aren't answering their phones anymore. Earlier, people wouldn't answer a long-distance number. Well, now, marketers and scammers can make their calls look like a local cellphone number.

What's frustrating to me is that I try to answer local numbers, whenever my kids aren't home. What if there's something going on with one of my kids. And I get very fed up when it's about a vacation deal or an extended warranty on the car. You have to remember that your patients are experiencing the same frustration. So when you are following up, they are not going to answer your phone calls, if they don't know the number.

When everybody first started emailing back in the late 90s, even your family would email you, right? How many of you get emails from your family now? We don't. We don't do that anymore because there are more personal ways to communicate with them. And email was taken over by spam. In fact, according to security firm Symantec, junk messages account for 49.7 percent of all emails.

Now the average chiropractor has a 10% open rate. If you email a thousand people, only 100 people are going to open it. That's really low, so email is not the most effective way to communicate with your tribe. Now, does that mean you should stop emailing? No, you should still do it.

If I'm emailing my clients, we have about a 60 to 70% open rate. However, if I'm emailing my list in general, my open rate drops to about 23 to 30%. It's still pretty good because I don't spam my audience. I make sure that I email great-quality content.

So if phone calls and email are not the most effective way to contact your prospects and clients, what should you do?

The magic of texting

"If your plans don't include mobile, your plans are not finished." ~Wendy Clark

During his keynote at the 2011 IAB Annual Leadership Meeting, Eric Schmidt, then CEO at Google, said mobile use was growing faster than all of Google's internal predictions. Two years later, Schmidt was even more emphatic, "The trend has been that mobile was winning. It's now won."

Mobile text open rates are as high as 98%, compared to just 20% of all emails. Also, text messages are opened within about the first 3-5 minutes. This is an incredibly effective way to reach and follow up with these leads. And the average time for someone to respond to a text is as little as 90 seconds whereas it's 90 minutes for an email.

If you calling your clients and prospects and are upset because nobody is answering, it's because you are not sending text messages. You have to implement text messages in your marketing and in your follow up. This can be unbelievably effective.

In the words of Nihal Mehta, "The mobile device has become our communications hub, our diary, our entertainment portal, our primary source of media consumption, our wallet and our gateway to real-time information tailored to our needs."

Most importantly, we are seldom separated from our mobile phones. We take them with us everywhere, which means that we can access mobile marketing in any setting. It's always on hand. So it's really important for you to learn how to tap into the power of mobile and use its unique traits to your advantage.

Action steps

"With our phones acting as supercomputers in our pockets, we can find, learn, do, and buy whenever the need arises—or the whim strikes." ~Lisa Gevelber

SMS is very effective way to communicate with your audience. Your prospects and clients are much more likely to respond to a text than a phone call or an email. So you need to add texting as part of your marketing strategy.

Make sure to visit tribeofpatients.com/bookbonus for extra content. There are a few other tips we share to improve show rate. You will love it!

Chapter 8

Leverage the Power of Retargeting

"Retargeting is one of the best ways to close sales that didn't happen." ~Neil Patel

Retargeting means targeting online ads at the same people again and again. It allows you to keep in touch with your prospective clients after they have left your website and offer them a chance to reconsider your offer. This is the third and crucial step in our process: always, always, always retarget.

Three types of audiences

"Repetition brings familiarity, and familiarity is the opposite of the unknown." ~Steven Levenkron

Whenever you are marketing, it doesn't matter if it's online, or on TV or radio. You are either marketing to a cold audience, a warm audience or maybe even a hot audience.

- **Cold audience:** people who haven't seen you or engaged with you. They know nothing about you and are unlikely to make a purchase right away.
- **Warm audience:** people who have engaged with you or your content in any way, which is measurable and trackable online.
- **Hot audience:** people who have visited your website and/or have supplied their contact

details. These are people that are ready to come and see you right now.

If you make an offer to your market, like a new patient special, it typically goes only to a cold audience. So how can you retarget people that you know have already been engaging with your content? That's what you want to do. You want to spend most of your advertising dollars targeting a warmer audience, and warming up that audience to make them a hot audience. You want to grow your warm market and then fish in that market.

For example, if you are looking for fish, you need to go to the ocean or a river with fish in it. If you go fishing in the wrong places, you'll catch nothing. Also, you are not just looking for fish but the right type of fish. For example, if you're looking for freshwater fish, you won't find them in the ocean. However, if you're looking for whales or sharks, you need to go to the ocean. Similarly, you need to know where to go to find the right type of audience.

Your target audience

"The size, scope and strengths of the campaign must be directed towards a specific target audience in order for it to be effectively executed." ~Germany Kent

Demographic targeting is a way to define your audience according to location, gender, age, family size, education, income, religion, ethnicity, and other factors. For example, you can define your target audience as women who are older than thirty, within a 10-mile radius of your office, is a homeowner, etc.

This will change for different offices that offer different services. For example, some of our offices are doing stem cell therapy, knee pain, neuropathy and so on. We wouldn't be targeting only women for these offices. For stem cell therapy, knee pain, and neuropathy, we would normally target an audience of men and women who are 50 or older. However, if you are a straight chiropractor, the majority of your patients are typically around 30 to 35 years and 65 to 70% of them are women.

Video retargeting strategies

"Before you start any business, you need to get your
target audience down pat.
Who do you want to serve?
Who will your product/service benefit the most?
Don't worry about the rest."
~Kevin J. Donaldson

We usually want to target our cold audience within a 10-mile radius. Maybe they are homeowners with income. We also want to do post engagements. These are people that have engaged with your posts or ads with likes, comments or shares. And you can use your database of prospects. For example, you can take all the leads from your screenings, build a warm or a retargeting audience and start showing them your videos.

If you are doing Google Pay Per Click advertising, you have to set up a Facebook tracking pixel on your website to retarget your website visitors. One of the first things we do with our clients is to make sure this pixel is set up. If someone goes to Google and finds you after typing in "chiropractor near me," he or she is a hot lead. If you get 3 to 10 such leads from Google on your website every day, you're probably missing between 50 and 100 leads a month that went to your website but didn't subscribe or call.

Let's say they went to Google, typed in "chiropractor near me." They found you, read your reviews, visited your website but they didn't call. That doesn't mean they are not interested. It could have been that the baby started to cry, the doorbell rang, the boss walked in—there are a thousand different reasons. If you're going to be distracted, it's going to be on the internet. There are tons of different reasons but they ended up on your website.

However, if you have a retargeting pixel on your website, you can tell Facebook to retarget anyone that has visited your website in the past 7 to 30 days (or you can go up to 180 days). You can use the pixel to build your retargeting audience. Then they will start seeing your videos the next time they are on Facebook. All of a sudden, as far as they are concerned, you are everywhere.

You probably had this happen when you went shopping online. You go to a website, and the next thing you know, you are seeing it everywhere. It's following you not just on Facebook but it's retargeting you on the different sites that you visit. That's what we want to set up for you or you can set it up yourself.

We also want to retarget people who view your videos up to 25 to 50%. If they can stop what they are doing to watch your video and know that they can trust you, it's huge.

For example, Dr. Travis posted his first video of a newborn getting adjusted. Then we set up a target audience of women, 35 and older.

Dr. Travis's next video was a patient getting adjusted. It was a short video, 2-3 minutes long and it was a girl

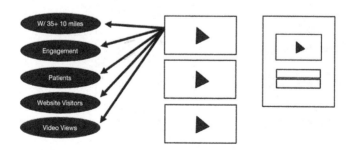

named Brittany and he said, "Hey, this is Brittany, and she's agreed to let be in our video today and if you've never been to a chiropractor, you don't know what we do, we're going to show you what we do in our office."

It was just a basic side posture adjustment and then Brittany talked about how much she loved the office and how long she has been going there. It was a great little video.

His third video was on bulletproof coffee or stress during the holidays. We did the same thing. The video came out, we retargeted all these people.

We can choose any database. We can target the level of engagement. We can target website visitors or video views. Then we take your video and target all these different audiences.

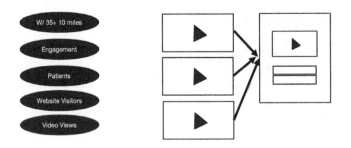

We target different audiences with these videos—women 30 years or older within a 10-mile radius, patient list, website visitors, video views, etc. Ideally, we want to grow the audience that is viewing the video (which is displayed below the video). That's the main audience we're trying to grow because if we can build that audience of people who know, like and trust you, it works very well.

Finally, we sent them all the people who viewed these videos to a landing page or a lead form or a survey, where they gave us their information if they wanted to come in for a new patient appointment.

Several years ago, I did a video with my son, Brenden. He's 13 now, so I think he was eight, maybe nine at the time. He was having severe headaches and the teachers were calling us, in the afternoon saying, "Hey, just letting you know, Brenden is sitting here with the trashcan in his lap again." He felt nauseated and had severe headaches, 4-5 times a week. I had a Chiari malformation type 1 and my older sister also had it. Though it's not hereditary, we wanted to get Brenden checked out. He should have been seeing a chiropractor this whole time but he wasn't—it was my fault.

We went to the pediatrician. He advised a CT scan, which was clear. The pediatrician said, "It seems to be a migraine. I want you to give Brenden 400 milligrams of ibuprofen at the onset of any headache." I thought, "Are you nuts?" There was no way I was going to give my son that much ibuprofen that often. I didn't want to treat only the symptoms.

So we decided to figure out what was causing those headaches. We took him to Dr. Walker who was my chiropractor here in my town. During the exam, he could tell that Brenden's atlas was shifted, "Look, there's no guarantee but I really think this is going to be it."

Sure enough, after a handful of adjustments, Brenden's headaches went from four, five times a week to once or twice a month. It was a huge difference. Brenden was too young to do a testimonial video. So he sat at my desk, kind of in my lap, and

I told a story and he interjected some of it. We ran this video as a testimonial video for our chiropractor in our town for about a month.

Surprisingly, we had two separate people stop us—the first time at a local restaurant and then at Walmart. Both times, it was pretty much the same conversation. They walked up to Brenden and said, "Hey buddy, how are those headaches?" He just smiled and said fine. Well, after the second time, I remember him looking up at me and saying, "Dad, I think I'm famous."

The point of the story is it happened even though we ran this one video in our town for a month without any retargeting like we do today. If you are doing these videos consistently, think of what it can do for you in your community.

You are going to be the one sitting at a restaurant, and people will be elbowing each other, saying, "Hey, look, that's the doctor who's always doing those videos." You build this almost star-like authority figure in your local community.

Another story I share sometimes is about a younger couple who owned a Dodge Chrysler Jeep dealership about 30 minutes south of us. They were probably in their early-to-mid 30s. I thought it was very impressive that they owned such a big dealership at their age. They were always on TV, always running commercials. I remember, I saw them at the mall one day. My first reaction was, "My goodness that's the couple who owns that dealership." Then, I stopped myself. I was like, "What, am I starstruck!" All they were doing was running commercials.

People will do the same thing to you. They will see you and recognize you. People want to go to somebody who's in authority and it puts you in that position.

Example 1: Anthony DiClementi

Have you heard of Anthony DiClementi? I recommend that you follow him. You would think he's a chiropractor. He wrote a book called *The Biohacker's Guide to Upgraded Energy and Focus,* he's got a membership site and he does high-level coaching. He

Anthony DiClementi was live.
May 13 at 1:15pm · 🌐

Use This YELLOW Superfood to Get Rid of Seasonal Allergies and Enjoy the Great Outdoors - Get Your Copy of My FREE BOOK now at www.BiohackersGuide.com

1.8K Views

👍 Like   💬 Comment   ↗ Share

does different videos about once a week or so, very much like what we teach.

For example, DiClementi has a video about a yellow superfood to get rid of seasonal allergies. In another video, he's at the beach with a kettlebell. He doesn't have his shirt on and he's totally ripped and the video is three exercises you can do with a kettlebell for your abs. He's in a different environment—at the beach. His shirt's off and he's using a different prop.

So he does different videos in different locations and it makes people stop and watch. In the video description of all his videos, DiClementi invites you to grab your coffee and provides a link to his free book that sends you to his website. He has built a seven-figure online business just by delivering these short videos and then sending the viewers to the top of his funnel.

Example 2: Dr. Josh Axe

Another great example is Dr. Josh Axe. He's a chiropractor. Some of you guys probably know his story. He was a pretty successful chiropractor and doing around 600,000 collections a year. In 2009, he founded draxe.com and a radio show.

2009: Founded DrAxe.com & Radio Show
2018: #1 Natural Health Site & $100M

go. Since starting his business nine years ago, Dr. Axe made over 100 million dollars in 2018. And he did it by posting good-quality content online.

Action steps

"Constant repetition carries conviction."
~Robert Collier

Review this chapter to set up your retargeting system and build your own retargeting audience.

If you need help, get in touch with us. Make sure to visit tribeofpatients.com/bookbonus for extra content.

Chapter 9

The Perfect Patient
Tribe Turbine™

"Customer service shouldn't just be a department, it should be the entire company." ~Tony Hsieh

Let's recap the three steps for better results with your social media marketing:

- The first step is to make viral videos that establish you as the go-to authority in your community.
- The second step is to use SMS/text messages to drastically increase your show up rates.
- The third step is to follow up and always be retargeting.

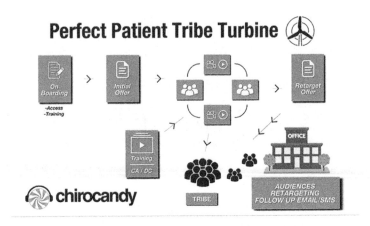

You start with a cold audience and turn it into a warm audience or even a hot audience and get those people to come in.

Our proven marketing system with a 95% success rate

"The only asset that can be kept safe from every threat and made to appreciate in value year after year is the relationship you have with your customers." ~Dan Kennedy

Our business, ChiroCandy Marketing, has developed a proven marketing system. The offices that allow us to do this verbatim get an easy 95% success rate. This

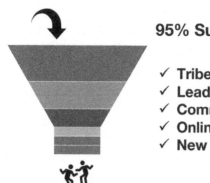

95% Success Rate

✓ **Tribe Targeting**
✓ **Lead info**
✓ **Commitment Survey**
✓ **Online Scheduling**
✓ **New Patient**

is our *Perfect Patient Tribe Turbine.* The lead comes in at the top of the funnel and gives us their information. They go through what we call a commitment survey. This is to find out how serious they are. Then they schedule an appointment online themselves and come into your office as a new patient.

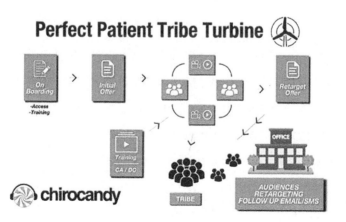

The onboarding process

This is the first step whenever we sign you up as a new client. You then give us access to your Facebook page and your Facebook ads account so that we can run your ads.

The training portal

Then we give you access to our training portal, which is being updated all the time. You have got a lot of other stuff that's going on so this portal is broken down into training for CAs and doctors.

The training for the CAs is about having a proper mindset. How to follow up with leads, how to use different scripts and so on. If seven out of ten leads don't show up, and only three out of ten are walking in the door, we need your CAs to understand that it's okay. Because if they have seven out of ten people say no, they may get discouraged. We don't want them to get discouraged. If you are a Major League Baseball player, and you strike out seven out of ten times but those three times you get a hit, you are getting paid millions. We want your CAs to have the proper mindset on how to follow up.

The training for you is how to create effective videos. We have a number of sample videos and a list of video topics.

The initial offer

This is whatever it is you want to do. It can be just a consultation or a workshop or a seminar. The initial offer will only go to a cold audience.

The marketing process

Once you start doing weekly videos, you can use the Facebook page app to upload them from your phone straight to your Facebook business page. You can do this on your own. However, if you are a client, you email our staff, "Hey, I added a new video." Some of our clients are very consistent. They do a video every Tuesday and we take that video on Tuesday evening, turn in their retargeting ad for the following week and rotate it.

All the people who watch your videos are your tribe. We build your retargeting audience of people that are watching your videos. We retarget your offer to these people who have watched your videos and they start to see you everywhere. They continue to see your retargeting offer until they come into your office.

We build out different audiences and do all the retargeting. We also have a fantastic follow-up system—a 3-month email follow up system. As we said earlier, about seven out of the ten leads may not come into your office. However, they did stop whatever they were doing to click on your ad and give their name, email and phone number. So we want to retarget them with a 3-month email follow up system.

Virtual CA

"Happy customers are your biggest advocates and can become your most successful sales team."
~Lisa Masiello

We're very excited about this new software, **Virtual CA**. It allows us to track your ROI and it has automatic online scheduling. It really is like a virtual CA. Your CA still needs to do a little bit of follow up, but for the most part, this software is doing all of the heavy lifting for you.

For example, a new office has four leads so they know it's about $5,400 in value. They have already closed one of those four leads, who has come in and signed up for care. It looks like they have lost a couple of leads but you can track them in the software.

Virtual CA also records all the conversations, including responses to the automated text messages. If someone calls, the software records the call so you can listen to it and see how your staff is doing. Everything is stored within the software. If anyone requests an appointment, your staff can respond automatically to the calls.

We have just started using Virtual CA. We tested it on a handful of our offices and it's working phenomenally well. It follows up with your leads until they schedule or fill up a survey. We are using it for tribe targeting and building your retargeting audience.

Not all of them do. That's okay. Your team can still follow up with them but the ones that do schedule online are an even better prospect. Then they become a new patient and come out of the funnel as a new patient. It works very effectively.

Action steps

"Whatever you do, do it well. Do it so well that when people see you do it, they will want to come back and see you do it again, and they will want to bring others and show them how well you do what you do."
~Walt Disney

Go to www.chirocandymarketing.com/tribe and check out our proven process that creates a tribe of followers who want your services!

Make sure to visit tribeofpatients.com/bookbonus for extra content.

Bonus Section

Section I

Beware of High-Priced Marketing Agencies

"Price is what you pay. Value is what you get."
~Warren Buffett

It's a fact that many Facebook marketing companies charge ridiculously high prices. They may charge anywhere from $1,500 to $2,500 every single month, whenever they're running your ads. They may not even be doing the same retargeting and follow up that we do.

Even if they are providing good service and you are getting good results, you are still losing a couple of grand out of your pocket every single month. And that's not even your ad spend; that's just their service fees. You can hire a CA for that amount. Seriously, some of these companies charge so much, you can actually hire an associate for what you're paying these companies. Personally, I think it's just ridiculous!

Most of these companies that charge such high fees don't keep their clients very long. A lot of our clients have been with us for over a year. Some of them have been with us for two or three years. We keep our clients for a long time. I'm very committed to the profession. We want to help as many offices as we can, as many people as we can, and as long as we can.

Our full service of Facebook and Instagram marketing

"The price of anything is the amount of life you exchange for it." ~Henry David Thoreau

1. Facebook/Instagram campaigns
2. Custom audiences
3. Custom landing pages with pixel

4. Dedicated support

5. CA and team training

6. Constant innovation

7. Follow up email campaigns

8. Follow up phone scripts

9. SMS scripts

10. And more

Set up

We set up your campaigns, custom audiences and landing pages with pixel. We set up a pixel on your website. We set up dedicated support for you and training for your CAs and team.

We are constantly innovating to provide the best possible results. These include follow-up email campaigns, phone scripts and SMS scripts. And we have the **Virtual CA software** that automates all the follow up for you.

We are constantly updating our training portal. It has 50 sample videos in the Facebook video marketing section to help you get content ideas. These videos are about 4-6 minutes each. We know you are busy, so we get straight to the point and give you some ideas and then let you run from there.

Pricing

At the time of this printing, our monthly fees are roughly 1/3 of what other companies charge.

Refer Three Get Yours Free

If you're happy with our services and you refer three offices to us, you don't even have to pay the monthly payment for our Facebook service, as long as those three offices are active with us. So we will do all of your marketing for free if we have three active referrals that you have sent in.

(We have got several offices that have been with us several years. They haven't paid us in several years because they have referred so many people to us.)

Action Steps

"Listen to advice and accept instruction, that you may gain wisdom in the future." ~Proverbs 19:20

Schedule Your Call

Let us show you our ***new, cutting-edge system*** for generating ***high-quality*** new practice members for your office! Discover a plan to quickly generate an endless stream of quality new patients! Schedule a call with me or one of our team members at www. chirocandymarketing.com/tribe.

Here, you'll find a short overview and the button to schedule your call. When you click on it, it will ask you a handful of questions and then allow you to pick a time on your calendar and schedule a call that works best for you.

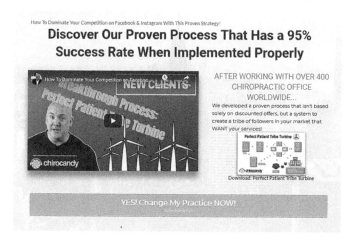

During the call, we can discuss how we can help you to use social media marketing to dominate your market. We will do our best to try to find something that works well for you.

If you can't find a time that works best for you, you can go to the ChiroCandy Facebook page facebook.com/chirocandy and shoot us a message.

Section II

Marketing Results Before You Pay!

Patient Visits Down? Watch this...

(Chiropractors & Functional Medicine Doctors)

Still open and seeing patients?

This is a very trying time for our nation.

Thousands of businesses are closing, schools aren't able to open, revenue is down across the board, family's stress is at an all-time high.

The best a doctor can do if patient visits are down is simple...

CUT EXPENSES & INCREASE

Its business finance 101: whenever revenue is down, expenses need to be too.

Now is the time to break up with the marketing agency that's charging $1500+/month.

I have been brainstorming ideas to better serve chiropractic as they serve their communities.

This has lead us to develop some strategies that we feel so confident in, we are putting our money where our mouth is.

To better help you serve your communities, we want to eliminate any financial risk that comes with working with a marketing company.

We won't charge you a dime until we book 10 patient appointments on your calendar.

(These aren't the tire-kicker, low quality "leads" other agencies provide)

These are REAL patients that NEED/WANT what you do!

The best part is you do not even have to worry about any ad spend.

This is perfect for offices that are:

- Tired of paying $1500/month+ for lead generation services
- Seeing a decrease in patient visits during the mass hysteria
- Just want to see more patients!

You can learn more and book a free strategy session with my team here: chirocandymarketing.com/get-started

Section III

Praise For ChiroCandy Marketing

"Hey there. This is Dr. Eric Mintz. I practice in West Bloomfield, Michigan, and I just wanted to give a quick shout-out to Billy and ChiroCandy for their marketing that they're doing for my office. We have been doing Facebook ads with them focusing on prenatal because I have a pediatric pregnancy focus in the office. If you're thinking about doing Facebook ads, don't hesitate, just do it.

The campaigns that they put on are amazing. The training is awesome, great customer service, so highly, highly, highly, highly recommend ChiroCandy, and

Billy Sticker for doing Facebook ads for your practice. Makes a huge difference, and I am looking forward to another great year with them."

Dr. Eric Mintz

"Hello, everybody. Dr. Tabor Smith here. I just wanted to shoot a real quick video for my good friend Billy Sticker, just an amazing guy. I have spent a lot of time with him masterminding seminars. He's always working hard for the chiropractic profession, one guy that absolutely loves chiropractors. Not only that, but he's extremely good at what he does. If I have any questions, if I need anything, if it's Facebook marketing, if it's developing the right pitch or the right wording, I can always reach out to my good friend Billy, and he knows exactly what I need.

If you're thinking about using his services, or maybe you already have in the past, and you already know, he's just phenomenal. I highly recommend him, and I just want to shoot that real quick video to tell you that you're making a good decision. All right, thanks."

Dr. Tabor Smith

"Hey guys, what's going on? Dr. Chad Woolner here, and if you are a chiropractor watching this video right now, looking for someone to help you grow your practice using Facebook ads and other marketing strategies, Billy Sticker is your guy. Billy Sticker is awesome. I've known Billy for quite some time now. And one of the things that frustrates me to no end that I'm sure you guys are seeing is your Facebook feed is probably blowing up right now with all sorts of self-proclaimed Facebook ad experts that are going to tell you all sorts of different things. And what I'm finding, unfortunately, I hate to say this, but 99% of them out there, they're not what they're cracked up to be.

Billy has been working with chiropractors for a very long time, and I have the utmost respect for people like him. I know several others who have been working with chiropractors, who aren't chiropractors themselves, but understand us. They get us, they understand what our frustrations are, they understand what our hopes are, what we really are after when it comes to bringing in new patients. He understands that the types of new patients we want aren't just new patients, but really, really good quality new patients.

Billy is great at what he does. He's a man of integrity. He knows what he's talking about. He's been in the trenches. He knows marketing. He's the best of the best. So I absolutely love Billy Sticker. I highly recommend him. If you're looking to grow your practice, contact Billy. If you're contemplating working with him, you will not regret it. He's a good dude and he knows what he's talking about."

Dr. Chad Woolner

"Hey guys, Dr. Dan McClimon here comi1ng to you from Beacon of Life Chiropractic in Royersford, Pennsylvania. We're about three months in with Billy and things are going amazing, volume's up, new practice members are up, our retention is good. We see a pretty good volume at this point. We're 400 to 500 plus visits a week, and our usual new practice members per month are between 35 and 55, something like that. In January we're going to see, with the people that we have on for next week as well as the last few days of the month, we're going to see over 90 new practice members.

Just the momentum that has come from the work that Billy and his team have done with Facebook has been incredible. The increase has been tremendous, collections are up and so the return on investment has been just phenomenal, and it's just been an absolute honor and pleasure to work with them. I mean, their team has been very helpful and accommodating with questions that we have, the start-up process has been very seamless, and it's just been a great thing for us.

So we've been, I've referred, oh, at least seven or eight of our friends in chiropractic, and I'm going to see a lot more of them this weekend. And the way that I think about it is that if this has been so great for us, I don't want my friends to miss out, or their families to miss out, on the blessings that have come to us from working with Billy. So that's about as honest as I can be. And I'm excited for you all to get to know Billy and his team. Thanks, guys."

Dr. Dan McCLimon

"Hi there. My name is Dr. Tyler Schwanz. I practice with my father, Dr. Jon Schwanz. The name of our practice is Rebel Chiropractic and we are located in Waterville, Ohio. And we couldn't be happier with our service with ChiroCandy since starting up. We have had one of the biggest months we've ever had in both just new people coming in, and even in high-quality people who are coming in, who are just really interested in what we have.

They let you do whatever you want as far as like the sorts of promotions that you're doing. We're not discounting anything, we're just getting our message out there. And the thing that rang true to me is that if everybody who drove by your practice knew exactly what you did, your doors would be knocked down. And that's what ChiroCandy has helped us do: get our message out there to the people, so we can just educate them. Not discount, but educate. So yeah, it's been a great experience. I would highly recommend it and you all should definitely write me down as a referral if you choose to go with them. Thanks."

Dr. Tyler Schwanz

"Hey guys. Dr. Andrew Oestreich here with Landmark Chiropractic. And today I want to share a little bit about our experience that we've had using ChiroCandy. And so it's been about six months since we first started using them. And really from the beginning, they have just made social media marketing so easy. From running the initial campaign to telling us what videos are going to work best here in our community, how long we should be running them, and how much we should be spending on these campaigns. Really, from A to Z, they've just taken a lot of that stress out of what we should be doing and just putting it into action, which has been huge.

And really from the beginning too, we have seen a ton of leads come in and we are reaching people in our community in ways that we've never done before. And it's really helped our practice a lot. And so if you are looking for someone to help you grow your practice and help you take a lot of that guesswork out of social media marketing, definitely reach out to ChiroCandy. They're really going to be able to help you answer whatever questions you have and really guide you in that right direction."

Dr. Andrew Ostreich

"Dr. Danny Governor from San Diego, California. I originally came across Billy through his podcast, and up until that point, I had built most of my business through word of mouth, but I had never really reached those numbers that I knew I was capable of reaching. So I decided to do some online marketing. And I was really nervous and I had no idea where to get started. So after speaking with Billy, we decided that Facebook would be the best place to get started. And I'm really glad that I did because he helped me get 50 leads the very first month that we worked together. And I was able to convert a lot of those to new patients. And now I've reached a lot of those numbers that I knew I could reach, but I never quite could get there.

So I highly recommend Billy. If you're thinking about getting started with Facebook marketing, he is the man to talk to. He's a man of action and he gives you a lot of value. And I just want to say thank you, Billy."

Dr. Danny Governor

"I just want to tell you first and foremost, Billy is the man when it comes to Facebook. We set up this great foundation through ClickFunnels to where people can get our information, get an opportunity to come in and get their spines checked, but not only that, to follow up with them on emails and information about what we do in the office. Then once we got that good foundation, he showed me how to create amazing content with just my phone. Then putting that content out there into my community and leading them to that page, it educates them more about what we do in those follow-up emails, which are out of this world, it was phenomenal.

Dr. Chase Dyess

"Hey guys, this is Dr. Emil Tompkins and I've been working with Billy Sticker for quite a few months now. And we have been marketing online for years in a number of different ways with varying levels of success. We've tried just about everything from our email to various funnels and I tried to create a lot of things myself. And we'd bring in a few people here and there and that was good and the exposure was good. But ever since working with Billy, we have had a lot greater success in our marketing. And when I say a lot, I mean leaps and bounds. Pretty much whenever I'm marketing with him, I have a steady flow of new patients so that I'm not really looking for other ways to market. We just started a neuropathy program in our office and right away, in about a week and a half, I had 20 or so leads of people expressing interest in being a part of this program.

So this is something that works. It's something that works. It's something that works well. Just like anything else, everything takes a little bit of work. But gosh, Billy does the hard stuff for us, so I really appreciate that. So just want to say hey, thank you. You have been tremendous for me and my practice and just thankful for the opportunity to work with you. Have a great day. If you guys are looking for someone to do marketing, Billy Sticker definitely is fantastic with the stuff that he does on Facebook. So thanks, guys."

Dr. Emil Tompkins

"Hi, my name's Dr. Steven Vincent. I'm a chiropractor in Amarillo, Texas. Everybody calls me Dr. Gunney, but I'm here to talk about Billy Sticker and his advertising through Facebook. It has literally changed my practice. We've started niche marketing just recently over the last few years, and the biggest market that we've been able to hit was our knee pain niche. Billy set it all up for us, and then just almost instantly we started getting leads just flooding our email.

And so, and these are leads that we have information on, that we can re-target later, but they're leads that our staff calls on and gets into the office. They've been easy conversions compared to a lot of the other Facebook marketing that we've tried. Billy's marketing seemed to be a little bit more streamlined, a little bit more focused, and so they have been way better Facebook leads than our others. So I absolutely, wholeheartedly recommend Billy Sticker for any of your Facebook marketing. Thanks."

Dr. Steven "Gunney" Vincent

"Hi, I'm Dr. Karl Baune with Power Chiropractic. I just wanted to tell you today, if you have not considered ChiroCandy, you should because we started with ChiroCandy two months ago, and over the course of those two months, we have generated over 300 leads and doubled our practice. It has been incredible, I couldn't tell more people about it. You guys have been a huge blessing. Get on it. Give Billy and Brady a call, they'll hook you up and they will be a definite asset to your practice. Thank you."

Dr. Karl Baune

"Hi, this is Dr. Jeff Wallace at Carroll Chiropractic and Sports Injury Center. We have been using Billy's program since May of 2017. After being in practice for about 20 years I have done every type of marketing possible. Over the past few years, the internet has become very powerful and we have brought in a lot of new patients from our website and testimonials. After utilizing Billy's program, the number of new patients from the internet has doubled and even tripled. Got to give you a big thumbs up, hat's off, Billy. This has been a total game-changer for us and life is great. Thanks again and I highly recommend Chiro-Candy to anybody that is thinking about it."

Dr. Jeff Wallace

"Hey guys, Dr. Matt Wink here. I want to talk about ChiroCandy and Billy Sticker. Not only do they have a great podcast, but I've been using them for Face-book advertising. Great support, great training in the beginning, teach you how to do all of the follow-ups. His team really helps you along the way a whole lot. I believe in the last six weeks, they have gotten us 136 leads. So if you are serious about getting into the Facebook realm of advertising, certainly recommend Billy Sticker and ChiroCandy."

Dr. Matt Wink

"Hey, what's going on everybody? My name is Dr. Dan Wallis. My practice is called Elevate Chiroprac-tic. We're in Fort Collins, Colorado. We've been using ChiroCandy for a couple of months now.

And I will tell you, before this, we had literally zero traction on social media. Nothing happened, nothing ever came from it, we had no action coming in. And I will tell you, now daily we get little notifications in our inbox of, "Somebody took action, somebody clicked, somebody watched our videos."

They've been saying, and it's true for us too, when we go to events, people are like, "Oh, I've seen your videos all over social media." My patients are like, "Yeah, I was flipping through this article and all of a sudden there was your video." It's amazing. I'm like, "Oh, this stuff's actually working for the first time."

These guys are phenomenal. They're easy to get in touch with. When I want something done or different or changed, our rep has been amazing. I would highly encourage you to reach out to them. What works for us can work for you. If you want to get this message to your community, this has by far been the most effective and efficient way that we've found. So check them out."

Dr. Dan Wallis

"Hi guys, my name is Dr. Chris Fowler and I practice outside of Jackson, Mississippi. I just wanted to give you a little shout-out about Billy Sticker and his advertising and what it's done for our office.

We've been using Billy for about six weeks now, and in that time, we've had over 300 people contact our office, interested in setting up the first appointment. And of those people, we've had about 150 actually set up prepaid appointments, so they paid for their appointments before they come in, and at this point, our practice is booked up for the next six weeks. We can't see another new patient until six weeks from now.

It's been a huge success for our practice. We've really enjoyed it. The people that are coming in are good quality patients, they're excited about care and we're having a high success of start rate as well. I encourage you, if you're looking to do some Facebook marketing or internet marketing to get in touch with Billy and talk with him a little bit about what he does and see if it's a good fit for you because it's been a great fit for our office. Thank you."

Dr. Chris Fowler

"Hey, this is Dr. Josh Wagner, creator of Patient Master in the Perfect Patient Funnel System for chiropractors with an endorsement and personal testimonial for Billy Sticker's Facebook ad service.

Billy has been running and overseeing my campaigns for exposure to chiropractors so they know the services I offer over the past two to three months. And in that time my cost per lead has gone down 75%. That's just incredible in and of itself.

But more so than that is the level of trust that I have in Billy and his responsiveness and then I know he's really there for me. Great turnaround time when I have questions and I know he's not going to disappear on me, which is easy to happen nowadays with all different services and coaching models out there. It's easy to not get the attention you're looking for.

So I endorse the experience I've had with Billy, both from the actual tangible monetary aspect, seeing a great improvement there and the relationship and the aspect of knowing he's there for me. If I have a question, if I need something, need something changed, he's always been there for me, and I know that's not going to change for other chiropractors.

So if you're looking to do Facebook ads to generate more leads and new patients coming into your practice, I definitely endorse working with Billy, giving him a try and seeing the results that he will get you. Thanks for all you do as a chiropractor."

Dr. Josh Wagner

"We own Higher Health Chiropractic in Grand Rapids, Michigan, and we developed SKED, but we also use ChiroCandy. And we found the experience we've been able to create for new people and new leads coming off of Facebook through ChiroCandy has just been really extraordinary and awesome. And how the two link together has been really cool and allowed us to get a lot more new patients from online, but they're coming in with a better experience right from the start. So we've had a great experience with ChiroCandy and highly recommend them."

Dr. Eric Kolwalke

"My name is Dr. Lewis Clark, and I've been working with ChiroCandy now for a couple of years. Previous to that, I tried some other Facebook marketing, and wasn't really good, wasn't successful. Then I got to working with these guys, and working with Billy, and with Brady. They really helped me zero in on the right ads, and really started getting consistent results. And now, I've been at it for two years, and we're still producing leads every month. They're good quality leads, so it's made a difference in our practice. So I recommend them highly."

Dr. Lewis Clark

"What's up, guys? Dr. Josh here. Yeah, I was just telling Billy when he came in, on total surprise notice, that I've had several different people run Facebook ads for me. And I literally have no connection monetarily to this guy, and I swear to you, it's crushing every other thing I've tried. It's doubled what the best guy ... and I swear to you, I've probably had five or six people do it. Doubling, not only leads, but people actually walk ... To me, leads are great, but when they actually walk through the door, and they're not just people that are here for the handout. They literally come in and are genuinely concerned about what's going on. So, night and day difference compared to everything else we've had, so absolutely...Sign up."

Dr. Josh Caldwell

"Hi, I'm Dr. Marc Nelson with Cadence Chiropractic out of Utah, and I've been with ChiroCandy for the last year now, and it's been fantastic. Since just yesterday, we've already pulled in four more leads. We consistently pull new patients, like way more than we've ever had before. I've worked with other Facebook groups before where we were paying $1,200 a month just for this guy to do the work, plus whatever the ad cost was. ChiroCandy is amazing. They saved us money and made us money. They're perfect at what they do. It's just awesome. They helped me with creating video content, everything. It's just been a fantastic experience. So yeah, I'd recommend ChiroCandy for sure."

Dr. Marc Nelson

"What's up, everybody? My name is Dr. Erik Brower with Innate Chiropractic, and I just want to give a shout-out to ChiroCandy. I love their services. They do a great job. We get many people coming into our office weekly and a few people a day. And even if they're not directly from a ChiroCandy referral, because we track all our referrals in our practice or where people are coming from, it's triple the number of people that are finding us online or we're meeting in the community are saying, "Hey, I've seen you around." Because just increasing our presence and our awareness in our community. And then they're finally pulling that trigger to come into our office and they're just listening online. So ChiroCandy is awesome. It's a great resource, great team, and just thank you guys so much."

Dr. Erik Brower

"I will tell you in my experience in our office since doing work with ChiroCandy, it's more frequently I walk into places in Boulder that people say they saw our video, saw you, they're at our events because they saw a video that myself or one of our team members did. Really awesome. So I've got to say check it out. He knows his stuff and really has his heart on helping chiropractors and helping more people have chiropractic care. And he really loves seeing patients get quality chiropractic care, so check him out."

Dr. Daniel Knowles

Section IV

Final Words and Parting Gifts

"A surefire way to predict the future is to take no action at all. When you do nothing, you get nothing."
~Pat Flynn

"All the magic happens outside your comfort zone, and in order to get to that magic you have to change." ~John Lee Dumas

Congratulations! You have reached the end of this book. If you are on your first read-through, it's time to start again from the first page and take action. Go through this book, review each chapter, one chapter at a time, and do every action step.

I hope you found this book valuable. There are tons of things here that you should be able to implement in your practice to help you reach your community more effectively with a message that they so desperately need to hear.

Section V

Schedule Billy or Brady to Speak

If you are interested in having Billy or Brady speak at an event, please email support@chirocandy.com

Section VI

Want To Write A Book?

"I Help People, Just Like You, Easily Write Their Book, Gain Instant Authority, and Leave a Legacy!"

According to the USA Today, 82% of Americans want to write a book.

I call BS on that!

I believe 82% of Americans want to have written a book.

*No one wants to **write** a book...!*

That's where I come in...

We have discovered a crazy trick that makes the process easy and painless...

To learn more, visit chirocandymarketing.com/book-vsl

Section VII

ChiroCandy Podcast

Make sure you check out the ChiroCandy show wherever you download podcast

It's available on:

- iTunes Podcast
- Spotify
- iHeart Radio
- Stitcher
- And More

Section VIII

Chiropractic Marketing University

How to use Facebook & Instagram Video Ads to grow a tribe of fans, and then turn those fans into patients.

Leads Leads Leads. Marketing agencies love to send you leads, but that doesn't mean anything if they don't show up for their appointments. Why is it that a discount offer works great at a screening or a health talk, but in a Facebook ad it just produces low-quality leads?

Two Words: Perceived Value.

If I had $1 for every chiropractor who's told me "I tried Facebook ads, but all I got were leads and no new patients", I'd be a lot richer. In fact, you might be telling yourself the same thing right now.

So, what's the problem?

- You had the offer.
- You got leads.
- You texted leads.
- You called the leads.
- You emailed the leads.

You did everything you're supposed to do and your Facebook leads still aren't scheduling or showing up for appointments – or when they do, they're just looking for a good geal. Not to start care.

So how do you actually get new patients from Facebook and Instagram?

Introducing Chiropractic Marketing University

After running Facebook ads for over 400 chiropractic offices, we developed what we call the Perfect Patient Tribe Turbine. The Process is simple...

Instead of blanketing an offer to everyone in your town, focus on building a tribe of raving fans. Then show them the offer and BAM... Instant high quality leads.

You can make Facebook videos educating people on what you do in the office, give advice on certain symptoms, or just give general health advice. What's awesome about Facebook is you're able to keep track of people that watch your videos and then target them specifically with ads. This strategy works great for any of niches in your practice:

- Chiropractic
- Pediatric/Prenatal
- Knee/Shoulder
- Thyroid
- Neuropathy
- Decompression
- Functional Medicine
- Weight Loss
- Stem Cell
- Laser
- And more

Why Use Facebook Videos?

Several reasons:

1. You can raise the perceived value of your office
   If all you do is blanket a single ad with an offer to everyone in your town, the only people that will sign up are the ones that want that discount! Just because they want the discount doesn't mean they want to start care.

   When you make educational videos for Facebook, you are showing the value that your office has

2. Set yourself as the authority in your niche
   Imagine, every time someone with chronic back pain turns around on Facebook, they see your educational videos on back pain, the see a patient testimonial, etc.

3. Build a relationship with people in your area to where they know, like, and trust you
   This is why screenings work so well. People start to know like and trust your

office whenever they're able to talk with you or your staff.

4. Find people that are suffering with specific symptoms you want to see in your office

There is not a way to target everyone in your town that has herniated discs. BUT... If you run a Facebook video ad titled *"The Truth About Herniated Discs"*, Everyone who has a herniated disc that Facebook shows that video to, will watch it. Now you have an audience of people in your town that have a herniated disc!

To learn more about this program, visit chiropracticmarketinguniversity.com